CROSSWINDS

Anita M. Krotz

CROSSWINDS

Poems by Anita M. Krotz
Utah Poet of the Year, 2017

Winner of the Utah State Poetry Society
Book Publication Award

◆

*The world is a book
and those who do not travel
read only one page.
– St. Augustine*

CROSSWINDS

Cover Art Conception: Anita M. Krotz
Cover Art Execution: Cheryl Walden, Graphic Artist
Photos: Public Domain, pixnio.com

Type Styles:
Covers: Arial and Arial Narrow
Section Titles: Arial Rounded Bold
Section Quotes: Snell Roundhand Bold
Poem Text: Helvetica

Published by the Utah State Poetry Society

Printed in the United States
ZDocs Printing
1084 E. State Road
American Fork, Utah 84003
http://www.zdocsonline.com

ISBN 978-0-9979386-1-6

Additional copies of **CROSSWINDS**
are available by contacting the author
at crosswindspoet@gmail.com

Acknowledgements and Dedication

I thank God and the Holy Spirit for the gift of life and for the teachings of Eckankar, the Path of Spiritual Freedom. I am grateful for inner guidance of the Living ECK Master, Sri Harold Klemp. Without this counsel and direction, I would have a much rougher road through this world.

Members of the *Valley Winds* chapter of the Utah State Poetry Society provided helpful critiques. Other poets have been invaluable in serving to fine-tune my work: Kathleen Campbell, Jon Sebba, Elaine Christensen, Lisa Gustavson, Lynne Benson, Louise Cook, Maurine Haltiner, and Patricia Peterson of *Hungry Poets*. Rita Bowles is awesome at organizing poetry gatherings. I'm looking forward to the retreat next year in England!

Apologies to any individual left off this list—Judy Johns was the first person to tell me the Poetry Society existed; I joined UTSPS because of her and have always been grateful she opened the door for me and helped find a venue for my concert. Thanks to N. Colwell Snell who planted the seed idea that I should send in a manuscript. It took a while, but I did it! Within the Society I have found lasting friendships and shared the joy and inspiration of writing poetry.

Kathy Clement helped with editing, organization, and feedback. N. Colwell Snell was a proofreader. Elaine Christensen encouraged my writing and was a reader at the October concert. Along with being a supportive and all-around good friend, Jon Sebba was an editor, proof-reader, and concert reader. I cannot thank him enough!

I'm grateful to family who have always loved me, especially my parents, Lea and George Krotz, other relatives, little ones now grown, Erica Sinik, Christopher Hoshek, and Lisa Reddy and their families.They played a part in this body of work. I dedicate this book to them. When one is single, family is often where you find it. To treasured friends, thank you for enriching my life.

I appreciate the judge, Beverly Monestier, for selecting my manuscript as the winner in this year's contest. Her recognition of my poetry collection has been a high point in my life. Judges in preceding years offered supportive commentary that helped improve the book: Rob Carney, January Gill O'Neil, Jeremy M. Downes, and Susan Elizabeth Howe.

Along with those already mentioned, I also thank Roger Johns, Paul Ford, Steven Leitch, and Gail Schimmelpfennig. Endless thanks to Kolette Montague for her special gift of humor and lots of email support while scaling walls and juggling lightning strikes. Thank you to many more who have helped in any way, small or large, in the production of this book.

Disclaimer

No one life could be fully contained within the pages of any size book. This volume of poetry about my life experiences contains but a fragment of a fuller story. It is a ride through time, and I have used poetic license to write some poems in which I made up details. This book contains both fact and fiction, truth and fantasy, also known as creativity or invention. Some poems are autobiographical and some are not. The reader can decide which is which.

I mention this to present an idea that reality is in the truth of what is being said, how it captures and presents the essence of an experience.

Some poems portray two precious cats that lived with me nearly twenty years. Zeke and Zena both passed on during the time I wrote this volume. I love and miss them more than I can say.

TABLE OF CONTENTS

SECTION III: THE LONG WAY HOME

PREFACE

◆

*Nobody has ever measured,
not even poets, how much
the human heart can hold.
—Zelda Fitzgerald, novelist
(1900-1948)*

Point of No Return

> *All journeys have secret destinations*
> *of which the traveler is unaware.*
> — Martin Buber

Halfway to Guadalajara on Easter Sunday,
the flight routine is standard. A coach cabin
attendant informs me of a gentleman
whose father appears ill, skin drained
of color like a faded memory. I investigate.

The man is a palette of gray and still as a stone.
"Your father doesn't look well."

> *"Mi padre está muerto,"*
> the son replies in a voice
> heavy and raw as winter.

"He's dead? DEAD?
How do you know that? Are you a doctor?"

> *"No, Señorita."*

I sprint to the cockpit, brief the pilots.
Two male crew members lay the father
on the galley floor, begin CPR.

Most passengers are unaware of drama
behind the curtain. Our Boeing 727 hurtles
through cloudless cerulean skies—a mother
and toddler read a story, happy birds
in a nest; a couple lean heads together,
eyes closed in a tapestry of love;
students returning from Spring break
are plastered to textbooks.

A wealthy doctor occupies Seat 4A
every week. He escapes to Vegas
Friday nights to play baccarat,
then slips home to Guadalajara
Sunday mornings. He is asleep,
but it is an emergency—I wake him.

Crew members are exhausted
from performing CPR. Our flight
and the elderly man have reached
the point of no return. Rigor mortis
has created limbs stiff as ironwood.
His dreams are now the breath of angels.
The doctor writes out a death certificate.

We strap the man into an empty seat,
shroud him with blankets and a blessing,
close the window shade.

As Inflight Leader, I must finish duties,
wait to squeeze the day from my eyes.
I have a mountain of paperwork—
          a holiday weekend
          a quarantined international flight
and one man whose destination
is beyond any he had ever hoped.

SECTION I

BACK SIDE

OF THE FRONT DOOR

◆

The journey itself is my home.
— Basho Matsuo

Trapeze

I come from red bricks and gray plaster,
towels drying on a rope clothesline
and a side yard where camellias hang
showy as women with ample cleavage,
where the olive tree snaps
like a switchblade in a windstorm
and kids play hopscotch on sidewalks
with bean bag markers.

I'm from blue cotton dresses
stitched with love, from a neighborhood
of open doors, friendly as a 24-hour deli.

I move to lobster bisque
ladled from silver tureens
by black-tied European waiters—
far from ravioli and schnitzel
with checkerboard cookies on Sunday.

The trapeze swings back
to childhood, a trompe l'oeil
painted on the ceiling of my mind.
Sometimes, I feel the weight
of my wings.

Two Hundred Billion Stars Away

I could never hold
the heel of my father.
I belong in the spiral
of the Milky Way.

He flies only as high
as a goldfinch.
His song strains
to reach a star—
an endless goodbye
bounces off heaven's arc
and is lost.

Storm clouds sweep
through autumn's altered air.
I am called to the nest
of twigs and grass.

Branches clash in gritty wind.
Boughs, laden with family ties
bend and twist. Hearts rim-full,
we sing his last song together.
The past stumbles upon itself
then stills.

I could never hold
the heel of my father.
From galaxies
generations away,
his earth was smaller
than a finch's tear.

Rainy Day Memory

Elementary school lets out
into a stampede of shedding clouds.
Third graders, just eight years old,
are as petulant as the rain.

Like a herd of goats in a roundup, kids
huddle under the asphalt roof overhang
or Disney-themed umbrellas.
One by one, mothers collect offspring.

Our family has only one car daddy uses
for work, so I know I have to slosh home,
my shoes swimming like fins.

Nancy, my friend, lives on the corner
of Tropical Avenue, the same street
as our school. Her mom comes
to pick her up and gives me a ride.

The car is slipping down the street
when I see my mother, walking
with a blue umbrella, bundled
in a red sweater with yellow boots—
a bright daub of primary colors
splattered on the gray canvas
of a wet sidewalk.
She had come four blocks to get me
since I didn't have my warm coat.

That slow-motion moment is locked
in time. More than sixty years later,
the love that burst from my heart
floods down streets of my memory
whenever I see children walk in the rain.

Horse of the Muses

The blood of mortal Medusa
created Pegasus.

Each night
the winged horse
opens my window
with a stroke of his hoof,
just as he released
the spring of Hippocrene.

At one time he carried
Corinthian Bellerophon
to battle.

Now he carries me.

I clutch the golden
bridle and slay my own
fire-breathing Chimeras
who roam dream worlds.

In the morning,

there are
hoof prints on the
bedroom carpet.

Fifth Grade

At ten years old, I'm taller
than nearly all the boys,
gangly yet graceful.
Our class files like a trail of ants
into the medical office to be weighed.
Nurse Barrett yells out pounds
as if it's the score of a game.

A girl named Cynthia, as wide
as she is tall, looks square,
like a block of Velveeta cheese—
partly from gorging herself on leftovers
from other kids' lunch pails.
She tips onto the scale,
covers chubby lips with pudgy hands
and whispers to the nurse in secret.
The nurse mumbles like she's toothless,
and the secretary scribbles it down.

I'm barely five-foot-four
and eighty-two pounds wet,
but my *out loud* weight
is the most of any kid,
boy or girl. It isn't more
than chunky lumpy Cindy,
but nobody knows that.

That linebacker chick may have
coronary disease or diabetes now.
        I don't care.
Part of my heart hurt so much that day,
it stayed in fifth grade.

In the End, It Is More Mysterious Than Life Itself

Woods behind Grandma and Grandpa's house
in Sun River are my playground. I am a brave explorer,
brave as my corgi who barks at forest shadows.

It is evening, yet daylight hangs long in the sky,
bright as a flashlight. I scamper like a mountain goat
to the top of a boulder and lie on my back. Hemlocks
are paint brushes on the easel of Montana sky.
My rock becomes a dapple gray Lipizzaner,
and the lake, the Pacific Ocean.

A bullfrog plops at water's edge, brings me back
to reality. I start home, weave through Ponderosa pines
tall as a ship's mast. Where meadow meets lake I see
a snow-white horse drinking. He turns, looks at me
over his left flank with a piercing lapis-blue eye.

A single spiraled horn juts from his forehead. Mane
and tail are iridescent, like bubbles. He paws
the ground, neighs with strength of the wind,
and gallops into weathered air—
all faster than I can breathe.

In the weeks that follow, Grandma sees my childhood
skip like a stone across the lake's mirrored surface.
She opens *Through the Looking Glass* by Lewis Carroll
and reads, *". . . Well, now that we have seen
each other," said the unicorn, "if you'll believe
in me, I'll believe in you."*

That summer I turn eleven is a storybook. In a flash,
I bolt from the carousel of youth. When the curtain
over my window of truth catches a breeze, I glimpse
myself still turning in circles, still looking for magic.

Set Free

1
Boar-bristles bend sideways
in the heavy hairbrush
as if the north wind
had flattened them.
Thin strands of silver hair
match the etched silver handle
that bears his mother's initials.

Before my best friend Billy
turns runaway teen,
he watches her stroke Medusa curls
one hundred times each night.

2
Attic boxes contain kitschy
remains of a life. From
the thorny thicket of family,
Billy takes only one thing.

3
His workbench vise
grips the tarnished brush.
A crushing blow
severs the handle.

His mother's thrashing tool
splinters into silver shards,
shatters Billy's underbelly
of resentment.

Clock with No Hands

Hardly a year passes that I don't think
of my parents on their anniversary.
She, a butterfly girl with silken wings
fluttering roads of youth in Lago Como;
he, a German boy,
striking as a blue cornflower.

Their tapestry is woven
with a Valentine wedding,
then her train crawls west
from Chicago to measured miles
of waiting. Marines land on Iwo Jima
beachheads. When frost rimes February,
my sister is born. The stork delivers me
a year later, at summer solstice.

Hardly a year passes that I don't think
of them on their anniversary—
one trudging through the vanishing mind
of Alzheimer's, one betrayed
by malignant ovaries—both a slice older
than I am now when thickets
tangled the future.

Yet everywhere in the old house,
music from their lives still
tangoes out transom windows,
pulses past a clock with no hands,
kindles memories of a girl
born in Italy and a boy who learned
to fly on silken wings.

Summer of Discontent

Poised on the fringe of the frontier,
are my great aunt and uncle—
saucy, fledgling adults.

She leans on the rail
by an unpainted door, mahogany hair
an arched cathedral, period style.
Wild tendrils escape the vaulted bun.
A soiled apron covers her muslin dress.

He swaggers on the stairs, callused hand
on hip, mustache, black and sleek as the fur
of a panther, defiant stare an irreverent psalm.
Rebellion rages on a handsome face.

A beret crowns my youngest cousin,
the fiery family rogue with a smile
as flashy as gold bullion. Gloved hands
shelter secrets, balance a bicycle upright.

Ancestral anarchy and simmering discontent
ricochet through memories of them.
They could be Etta, Butch Cassidy,
and the Sundance Kid.

Their rough-hewn kitchen table
with one short leg, wobbles.
A pot of corn soup tilts yellow,
smells savory. Dusk breaks bread.
Lard sizzles in the cast iron skillet
as plundered buffalo splatters bloody brown.

Rebels all, they are like flies that buzz the window,
thieve the silence, unaware the flight to freedom
is a foot away.

Aftershocks

Max steps outside before shutters
blink open, lies on the grassy bank.
Swim trunks are dark as wounds he carries
under his skin. Grief's bone-raw, biting
as morning lake water. By the time
sharp light stabs air, he has carved the lake
from our bank to the far shore and back.

Seasons at the cottage always wipe away
the end of school when my cousin Maximus
and his best friend Matt are ripe to skip stones.
Now my cousin's core is hollow, insides
scrambled like radio waves.

Students were as easy to pick off
as low-hanging peaches when bullets
reshaped bodies, sprayed Mr. Helman's
history class. The shooter's thin-trap
mouth sealed shut to any emotion.
Teachers tackled him, but not
before blood spread across Matt's
swim-team shirt. Blue school letters
turned sticky, deadly purple.

Max has the look of a young Roman god,
walking around bare to the waist,
jeans slung loosely on his hips.
Summer girls melt like cotton candy,
pose in Adirondack chairs,
hope for a glance from aquamarine eyes.
The snow-globe lives we share, once crackling
with energy, are now shattered. The Max I know
is missing, folded in on himself.

Unfaithful Moon

Well beyond midnight, moonlight
weaves through windows, embroiders
a double cross-stitch, slants
off silver threads of tapestry.

Drops of sherry glimmer
on beveled edges
of a Waterford goblet.
Grandmother sips—
tastes vinegar in her mouth.

Unbending as linen thread, a grimace
frays her face. Anger stitches
the back of her throat. Needlework
normally settles her, but tonight,
the lunar pull unravels taut cloth.

The moon abandons the sky.
A fringe of frustration drapes her shoulders.
Steeled, she waits in the silent parlor,
mulls over her mangled marriage.
Her hand flattens the tapestry,
feels crewel knots
in the weft and warp of the fabric.

Loud as a drunken quarrel
Grandfather blows in, air around him
shadowed, scent thick with guilt.
He scatters scissored words
over Grandmother's seams of rage.

About-Face
Inspired by Dorianne Laux's *Face Poem*

Your newborn suckling face. Spherical
sitting-between-our-parents cherub face.Toddler
offering-me-toys-through-bars-of-my-crib-face.
Your willing-as-a-kitten-to-play sister face. Jealous,
grandma-loves-me-more bludgeon face. Your
garish-crayon, Revlon-caked, venom-secreting
high school face. Eye liner thick as tar, hair-ratted-
as-a-thicket face. One gold earring away from tacky
face. Heady doctor's wife, better-than-you, tractor-claw
face. Your mother's-milk-hope-for-us face fades
to stake-in-my-heart callous face. Rasping teeth,
blood-sucking lamprey face. Your acid-green bitter-winter
divorced face with brutal, cyanide-laced, thistle-tongued
mouth. Your nettle-nosed, bracken-eared, carnivore-lipped,
black-widow-eyed ovarian cancer face. The festering-flesh
sickly gray smear of it, the lumpy tumor-invading gnarl of it.

Your sudden steep shock of a sallow face
     faces my grooved-jaw, jolted-precipice face.
     My stretched-skin, arsenal-disarmed, hope to,
     want to, trying-to-forgive-you face, vaulted eyes
     towering over beech-white, timbered,
     silent-as-a-tree face. My anxious, fearful,
     sorry, salt-stained face, wounded, wishing
     it were yesterday, Uzi-lowered, let's-try-again face.
     My feverish, frightened, buried-in-the-pillow
     caterwauling grief face, faces your purple-skinned
     necrotic-casket face.

My sudden steep shock of a sallow face, knowing you
     are my-only-sister and I-love-you-will-miss-you
     face, drops a tear-dampened rose beside your
     cemetery burial face.

Last Rites

The moon pulls the tide,
tugging emotions, crashing
against the page.
They scatter.
Chambers of my heart swell,
stretch like elastic, rebound,
slap memory.

This morning, after coffee
and a fried-egg sandwich,
I walk a short block to the church.
An easel holds your picture,
weak smile, chemo-bald head
covered by a wig. Crystalline
Ave Marias rain down.
Fuchsia roses ramble across your coffin.
Twelve doves release your spirit.
A hawk swoops.
Two white feathers fall,
one for each daughter
you leave behind.
They don't know
the magnitude of your cruelty.
I can only smear staccato bursts
of a pen in my journal,
your eddy of darkness
so swirling, it screams.

I want my anger
buried with you.

Flaming Candles

Summer of 1969, I came of age.
Youth would be over
faster than my rebellion,
and fall term would bloom
sooner than fate. Before we headed back
to college or forgot how to make memories,
sorority sisters and I wanted to party.

Six long-haired bohemians
set out from Haight-Ashbury
for Max Yasgur's dairy farm
in the Catskills.
Skinny as exclamation points,
we piled into Lizzy Pratt's
flower-powered van.
Tie-dyed t-shirts flared
over hip-hugger, bell-bottom jeans.
Mother worried I dressed like *Barbarella*
but my curves
were smaller than parentheses.

Driving to Woodstock,
we recited Ginsberg and Ferlinghetti,
radio blaring like a siren
to keep us awake—The Beatles,
Joplin, Jimi, The Grateful Dead.

We knew lyrics
to all the songs
as well as we knew each other.

Six arteries
feeding the heart of friendship.
I was an unleashed, untamable gazelle...
Maddie, our lawyer-to-be,
sharp and black as obsidian...
Lucy, ablaze in ginger-colored hair,
on birth control for five years...
Emilia, our widening spiral
of spirituality and Pratt,
the psychologist who helped us
chase down the hoodoos.
Rah Rah Rachel was happiest
in a noisy flock.
When Creedence began to rock,
she was skinny-dipping in Filippini Pond
while belting out *Born on the Bayou.*

A half million strong, we huddled
in Max's rain-muddied field
that weekend, names written
on the wind. Life was never again
as loud or as rife with possibility.
It was the end of the sixties,
nearly the end of our resistance.
College was a rose-pink dawn
before the wicks burned down
and our flaming candles
began to flicker.

SECTION II

STREAMING THE WORLD

◆

*I have a trunk
containing continents.
— Beryl Markham, adventurer
(1902-1986)*

Escape

Imagination is the highest kite one can fly.
—Lauren Bacall

Brazilian cloth kites
samba the shoreline
until they are airborne,
tugging against string
wrapped around driftwood.
They dip and flutter like caged laundry
on a line, then puncture the sky
with a spectrum of plumage
in the shape of a Hyacinth Macaw,
a Yellow-chevroned Parakeet,
Red-breasted Toucan,
and Grass-green Tanager.
Grey gulls soar closer,
dive with angry squawks.

Wind carries the silk-winged
flock higher. Aerial twirls and pivots
become a choreographed dance.

A sudden gust snaps tethers.
The kites hover, then begin
to glide home in the direction
of the Amazon.

Tails flit.
Wings rise like the phoenix,
flap for freedom.

Feathers on the sand catch my eye—
luminous shades of cobalt, saffron,
vermillion, emerald.

Feral caws
fade in the distance.

Career at 35,000 Feet

Do not follow where the path may lead.
go instead where there is no path
and leave a trail.
— Ralph Waldo Emerson

Wind shear flips the MD88
like a paper airplane. I stare at frigid water
of the Columbia River Gorge. Eerie silence
fills the cabin except for whispered prayer.
Deplaning in Portland takes longer than usual,
due to passengers shaking the captain's hand.

A beggar on a bridge in Bangkok
has just two limbs. My coin tumbles
into his bowl like a living appendage.
It lights his eyes, bright enough
to cripple the poverty.

Enroute to Guadalajara,
an elderly man dies.
The son shrouds his father's face,
grips his old suitcase,
plastered with expired visas
and the last stamp
in a passport. At the layover hotel,
a single flower adorns a terra cotta vase.

Lost in Dublin on a rain-drenched afternoon,
a gaze of green on the side of the road
flashes toward the Volkswagen van's window,
tips a hat. He points.
Two blocks to Mrs. Cronin's Bed 'n Breakfast,
he announces in heavy Irish brogue,
then disappears fast as a Leprechaun.

Antigua churches crumble
when the earth shakes,
expose passageways that maze
between convents and monasteries.

Sermons assault preteen girls
whose fetuses cloister tunnel walls
that weep with platitudes.

Antonio is billboard-handsome,
bronzed by the Algarve sun.
He advertises spicy Mediterranean cuisine,
but is bland as unseasoned bouillabaisse,
limp as a Lisbon lie.

Bora-Bora, Moorea, Huahine,
form an archipelago necklace—
emeralds surrounded by liquid aquamarine.
From the night sky,
they are yellow sapphires
nestled in ebony velvet.
A tattooed Polynesian waiter,
dressed in smiles and a sarong,
serves coconut mai tais.

Orville and Wilbur
made streaming the world
a possibility. I thank them
for the déjà vu in Paris,
for Giovanni in Tuscany,
for the sleigh ride in Moscow,
and the candlelit dinner
in Buenos Aires.

Parselmouth

One who speaks the language of snakes . . .
—J.K. Rowling, *Harry Potter*
and the Chamber of Secrets

Captain, presumptuous and cocksure, the *Sorting Hat*
places you in *Slytherin House* where cunning is admired
by serpents just like you.

With a cold-blooded hiss, ruthless jungle invective
pollutes airways. There's gravitational lure
as our plane orbits the earth, but my answer is no,
I won't go out with you.

Epaulet stripes are rank markings
of your venomous rattle.
Like a common adder, you hide under a rock,
then sidle down the cabin aisle with a basilisk gaze.
Viperous, you slither through cockpits,
coil in diamondback posture.

You shed your skin, litter lounges
in King's Cross Station—with no boundaries
at all. Forked tongue licks the air searching for prey.
You drop from cover, strike, unhinge your jaws
and swallow whole.

Give me a harmless garter snake,
not a far-ranging cobra who rears
to strike and spreads his threatening hood.

    I said no.

Go back to the jet stream swamp
where your heavy green anaconda mate waits.

Or did you forget that constrictor?

Ritual

Turbulence torques our bodies.
Captain's orders: remain seated
for the duration of the flight.

Sagal and I
are strapped into the crew jumpseat
on a 737. Divided from the cabin,
it's a confessional, sometimes
a therapist's couch. Her story
begins in Africa. The narrative
is a vortex. She says,

> I must seal sorrow in a raffia basket.
> It lies scarred and hidden
> under a mudcloth shawl
> decorated with ebony beads.
> Dread clogs my throat,
> as red and angry
> as my sister Awa's blood.
> I finger a tiger's eye amulet
> to ward off evil.
>
> Running faster
> than monsoon winds
> can scatter sand,
> I steal eastward
> toward Mogadishu,
> leave my poor village
> sleeping. It is wet season.
> The sky is ragged
> with nimbus clouds.

Next full moon I would marry—
a groom chosen for me by elders—
a Paleolithic man. I am to be plucked
like a clove to oil his petals.

My sister Awa struggles ferociously
when it is her turn, our mother
too poor to afford anesthesia.

Older Somalian women squash her
like a bug under a fingernail.
Each slash, a strafe of pain—
razored—until circumcision
is complete. Acacia thorns
sharp as needles stitch her up.
Awa's fractured future is fate.

I stay off main roads,
drink from courtyard prayer fountains,
rest in gardens
that wrap arms of peace
around Mosques.
My feet are sails
that catch a quick wind,
anchor me in the asylum
of the sea. Salt water
is the same color
as Awa's tears.

A lifetime later we land without incident
in New York. Violence of aircraft turbulence
will never again crack me against a fuselage
the way Sagal's story
cracked open a strongbox
of security
in my safe little world.

It's All for the Birds

Last stretch of a puddle-jumper three-day—
hoping it's as caramel-macchiato sweet
as my SeaTac Starbucks.
I want that shaky-kneed caffeine rush
on my leg home.

> The only similarity turns out to be
> hot, steamy, frothy.

Three songbirds nest at the bulkhead,
luggage piled around feet like incubating eggs.
Ladies, I begin, *let's find overhead bins
or I'll need to check your bags.*

Grey-blue Nuthatch advertises her territory
in loud song, fluffs feathers, stiffens her tail,
thrusts a strong beak.
> *It's fine here,* she trills.
Federal regulations, I hoot, smiling.
Titmouse chirps in with a quick,
> *We're okay.*
Mockingbird
> mimics, mimics.

It's a Darwinian moment. Crews are trained
in *survival of the fittest,* so I don't shriek
or need talons. Calm and sharp-eyed,
I fly to the hunt, feathers adapted for silence.

Lucky the birds had Snowy Owl to serve them
instead of Turkey Vulture, Harpy Eagle,
or worse, Carrion Crow.

October Cups a Sparkler in My Hands

Brisk fall, San Diego layover, rented car,
me dressed in Western Airlines' bright-red
Flight Attendant blazer and navy skirt,
my sweetheart in blue suit and Pilot wings.
I'm an untethered balloon as we drive
to the address on the back of a pale photograph.
The weathered house spreads like a brood hen.

An elderly seaman, ports-of-call eyes,
answers the ring. I tell him my story, show him
the photo. Dad returns from the Marine Corps
in '46, a rainbow in his heart; my parents
buy this house. Dad carves my sister's
and my name and birth dates in the steps
on the back stoop—February, '47
and July, '48.

If still there, could I take a picture
to show my sister's children?—Family history.
The man leads us through the house
to the back door. My breath quickens
like colored flames. Two steps down
to a scruffy lawn—there, chipped but visible,
our heritage.

The moment, beautiful
as a piece of Point Loma driftwood,
bookends the day. Leaves
skip the steps like fingers
skimming a keyboard. Childhood
is a brief burning sparkler—
my sister and I playing in this back yard,
Grandma watching over us
as she probably still does.

Alaska Is a Grizzly

The cavernous maw of Anchorage
encroaches upon Alaska's wilderness
where animals outnumber humans.
Nature's honeyed beauty of fireweed
contrasts with a wild and explosive town.
People maul pristine habitat as Ursa Major,
once visible against onyx wilderness,
fades into pollution.

Our aircraft vectors through russet strands
of sunrise. Bull moose, as common a sight
as lodgepole pine, roam taxiways.

Under a crust of early morning sky,
a pet Samoyed is dragged from its leash
like a stuffed toy by a pair of arctic wolves.

Just beyond city streets, bears wade
through white water of salmon-swollen rivers.
Drawn to spawn, flashes of silver leap upstream,
are gripped by powerful jaws. Water
sheets off coarse fur like it would from an oil slick.

A protective sow rears on circus-bear hind legs.
Heavy hump of shoulder muscle
quivers and shakes like a minor earthquake.
Searching for ripe berries,
she crosses an asphalt tongue
of civilization. Slow gait becomes a snarling rush
as dirt pools raspberry-red in a careless hiker's tracks.

Aircrews lumber to Simon and Seafort's
where, like bears, we dine on chinook—
innocent of worn trails, broken brush,
and scattered scat a block away.

Gnawing Reality

Miles Davis spills
from the jukebox at Holland Bar.
A many-tongued manx, notes
lick the sidewalk, sweet and sassy
as Sloe Gin Fizz.
Sated with music from *Cats,*
I purr, walking arm in arm
with my love.

A New York City theater week—
musicals, dramas, Broadway, off-Broadway,
everything thespian—we haunt playhouses
like Hamlet's ghost. Unrestrained libertines,
we make a *Tom Jones* production of food.

Two-thirty a.m., sleep-deprived,
we turn a corner, escape taxi taillights
and city-thrum of 42nd Street.
Quiet engulfs us. Pleasure shifts.

     Sudden madness.

A brown wave sweeps the street,
clicks, scurries, changes direction—
a colony of eighteen-inch rats,
bald tails snaking.
Blood-spattered Macbeth
or Dracula
with glinting fangs
could walk onto this stage
unnoticed.

     Dread enfolds like fog,
     births bone-trembling terror,
     traps us in night's dark cage.

Where are the cats?

Alps of Adversity

It is just a small light,
a mere speck against
the night. A stranger
bivouacked in a sleeping bag
on the southeast face
of the Jungfrau.

From the warmth
of the inn, I watch
through a window,
marvel at his bravery.
Alone on the mountain,
trusting pitons
and carabiners to hold
in buffeting winds.

I imagine him—young,
rugged, perhaps bearded—
a solitary sort who
challenges himself.

My mountains don't involve
equipment, but I'm on a ridge.
One misstep and the ropes
won't hold. I could easily
slip into the abyss
of blackness, a chasm
so deep I'll never be found.

Perhaps the climber
will show me a toehold,
lend me his light.

Yellow

Summer migrates to the Dordogne. Footloose
in Southern France feels like a familiar language.

Sun blisters, air blankets. Blazing sunflowers
tower in fields with joy, infusing senses
with sweetness—their saucer faces,
like haloed cherubs, decant honeyed light
over hedges bordering
Plum Village Buddhist Monastery.

They bow, then listen when monk
Thích Nhất Hạnh gives dharma talks,
share silence when sisters have tea.

On meditation walks I revel
in yellow-drenched abundance and a heady scent
of lavender. The only accompaniment—bee music
and wing-snaps of sparrowhawks.

Baritone sky, low-pitched in blues,
is a perfect backdrop for diva blooms.
Center stage, each sings an aria.

A woman asks me to take her picture,
meadows behind, a tapestry of tawny
and amber. Without her saffron-brimmed hat,
she could be a chameleon, flaxen hair
melding with sunflowers' sturdy stalks and heads.

By the time I leave the Dordogne's
steamy summer behind,
my crackly edges have peeled away
to an inner layer of pure peace.
In days since, I remember
how to be sunshine and butter,
lemon and gold.

Call of the Celts

Summoned by strength of a taproot
to the Emerald Isle, I breathe green,
am heady with rain and misted mountains.

Cliffs of Moher stand rampart against the brunt
of Atlantic storms smashing rocky shores. Enya
plays on the radio. My Fiat pushes along ribboning
backroads, over patchwork pastures and bony fields,
past stone-framed farms and paddocks.

I round a hill, smell burning peat, see a caravan
of gypsies. Horses graze on moors. Needing directions
I slow, am surrounded by faces the color of beetroot.
Prybar hands snap door handles, thrust
through windows, pound trunk and hood. Fingers
grab luggage filled with Waterford crystal, a gold
Claddagh ring, Aran-knit sweaters, and Irish linen.
They rock the car, want to roll me
like their barrel-roofed wagons.
          You have money? Food?
My camera, heavy with telephoto lens, moves
with vulpine deliberation from the seat beside me
toward a slick-fingered Rom. I grab it back,
gun the engine, take off like a pistol shot.

Firing of my heart triggers a race over crisscrossing,
unmapped rural roads. I stop for a dinner of mutton
and potatoes when air smells of Guinness, grateful
that kissing the Blarney Stone brought me good fortune.

The land of Heaney, Shaw, Beckett, and Yeats
will always have *a terrible beauty*
that haunts recollections of stony fields,
yet brings blinding brightness
like the inner chamber of Newgrange.

Rising Sun

The land springs from the shogun's sea,
     like a thousand leaping tigers
     vaulting toward their destiny.
Silent spirits shatter threads
     of antiquity as high C-sharps splinter glass.
     Shinto practice spreads

sacred power through
     dragon dynasties. The imperial palace,
     carved with ivory hands, lies in full view
of pagoda coastlines.
     Thrust of the sword gives way
     to Buddhist shrines.

Land of the Rising Sun
     kabukis snow across a half-moon bridge,
     delicate as a geisha. Spun
silk orchids cascade down the Emperor's gate,
     splash kimonos of the courtesans.
     Origami cranes migrate

like brush strokes on a vellum scroll,
     circle the summit of Mount Fuji,
     then nest in a carved jade bowl.
Ancient samurai warriors die,
     breath braided among Japanese quince,
     brave as the bonsai

tree conscripted to scale.
     Haiku silhouettes sketch
     perfect cherry blossoms, frail,
yet fragrant as ceremonial tea.
     Showers of solitude line the road
     to enlightenment, the zen of satori.

Ten Cents a Bloom

She squats in a square of shade. Heat shimmers
in waves above sidewalks. Light swarms with color.
Jasmine and incense clot air. Horn-heavy sounds,
mooing, barking, clanging of bangles on wrists
surround her barefoot stem of a child, who eats dhal
from his mother's mustard seed fingers.

The caste system carves society—a billion people
fall like whittled shavings into social ranks,
layered through time to form the pyre of untouchables.

Mother and son sell flowers: 5 rupees a blossom.
The boy's transparent eyes blow through my heart.
I bring him oranges and mangos from the morning buffet.

When day tumbles to evening, I imagine
they move home to a patch of grass with a roof
of leaves. Perhaps they get milk from stray cows
or goats that roam free, collect dung to use
in cooking fires. Will he always taste hunger,
always speak the language of the needy?

The boy thrusts a violet crocus at me as I leave
the gated hotel compound for the last time. I pass him
a chocolate muffin—his eyes, two petals of happiness.

How easily I fit back into my life. No ball and chain
of poverty or fetid pollution cover my neighborhood.
No macaque monkeys shriek and bare teeth
as summer spills into fall. No stray dogs
with swollen teats roam streets. I shape
and reshape memory. I see the boy, his fierce face
a lotus flower of joy, his twinkle, a string of stars.

Le Mont-Saint-Michel

Ghostly echoes of Gregorian chants
reverberate through time, haunt
the thirteenth-century abbey,
overflow the bay. Benedictine monks
cloister the Gothic fortress, labor in worship.

Kyrie Eleison christens the cathedral
with praise, arches upward to touch
the purple hem of heaven. Stained glass
melts umber and azure across cold granite floors,
polished smooth by robes and sandaled feet.

Peal of bells,
a call to prayer.
Dawn and dusk,
the silver cord
of psalms trails
over cobblestones
washed by tears.
Whispers of priests
breathe through vaults,
hover over tides like a mirage.

Through mist, a shepherd,
older than ancient melody,
intones hymns for sheep—
sky his altar, clouds his apse,
salt his incense, mountains
his buttress, nature his monastery.
        With wind-whipped devotions
he serves his flock. Bleats
harmonize with the murmurs of monks
drifting from shadows, rise
like hands extended in ecstasy.

Wake of the Wind

I have not forgotten how the wind
held your voice and the air
around you felt like silk. Your song
burst over the Pont Neuf like fireworks
crossing stars. Laughter rippled waters
of the Seine.

Every inch of you, Parisian, artisan,
long and lean in cashmere and jeans,
as if you stepped out of an Armani catalog.
I was completely unmoored.

Spring and summer
were an Impressionist painting,
a canvas of color
and brushstrokes.

Mornings at the Sorbonne,
afternoons, the Louvre,
evenings in constant motion
like dancers at Moulin Rouge.
Sundays were croissants and espresso.
Wrapped only in skin, we watched lovers
cross the Île de la Cité, pass below
your apartment window.

In fall we made promises
that smoked the ground like fog.

Today, I stand again on the ancient bridge.
Memories rattle up and over arches.
The wind is made of bones.

The Letter

It came on a Tuesday this April.
Curlicue writing, but not calligraphy—
beige envelope, bold black ink. Envelopes
change color, but never the ink; always black,
always a fountain pen.

Letters never come in July when I was born,
never in June or December to celebrate
other family birthdays. Letters come only
in April, always in April. Postmarks from
Capri, London, San Francisco. A friend
lives in the heart, she remembers.

Teardrops on the beige envelope
blur the ink. The worn and slender
letter opener—pearl handle, brass edge—
slowly splits the beige-ness . . .
at once a knife wound, at once comforting.

Tears subside. Pink box under the bed,
this letter joins the others. Thirty-two
letters from thirty-two Aprils. She never
forgets. She shared the heart-searing
pain, and she never forgets.
Across the miles we celebrate Sadie—
precious—pretty—Sadie—
sweet—soft—pink—Sadie.

The promise of Sadie, the firstborn.
The memory of Sadie, the stillborn.

SECTION III

THE LONG WAY HOME

◆

Writing poetry
is like finding your way home
and you didn't know you were lost.
— Dianne Lockward,
The Star-Ledger, 26 April 2003

Love Bears Me Home

Not all those who wander are lost.
—J.R.R. Tolkien, *The Fellowship of the Ring*

Free from career,
I fall from the firmament,
trade crew wings
for garden clogs and gloves.
The ground swells
with slender shoots of carrots and kohlrabi,
beets and broccoli, radishes and romaine.
Summer bursts forth with tomatoes
the size of softballs, scarlet runner beans,
and fat ears of sweet corn,
the color of sunshine.

Harvest season
turns to coppered autumn.
Air tastes of concord wine.
From the porch swing
I watch sandhill cranes migrate south.
Winter pours its purity
and my footprints are lost.

When spring contrails
streak the wind, gypsy wanderlust
becomes as relentless
as westerlies.
Something in my blood
wants the sky. Inside,
still tall and twenty,
tan and toned,
I fly away, leave domestic life

with its mullioned glass,
and glide under the moon,
untethered as a Zeppelin.
Painted days spiral,
carry me
to the Great Nebula of Andromeda
and back.
I know there are more years
behind than ahead.
The travel trance sorceress,
out of spells, releases her hold.

I spin like a compass,
let go of Myanmar,
cross the Mariana Trench.
Greenland's ice cap
melts into Baffin Bay.
Time stretches, dilates,
drops to ash. A train to Le Mans
pulls out of Montparnasse.

This world is a Punaluu Black Sand Beach,
a Tanzanian sun, a Swedish polar night.
Motion trysts with miles, until I touch silence.
When my heart is nearly pumped dry,
a guardian spirit protects me
from the precipice.
New as innocence, old as silk,
the hourglass of longing empties.
Love bears me home,
skin dusted with freckles,
brunette tendrils tinged with gray.
The nomad in me
is swaddled in quiet comfort,
cradled in memories.

Fly Away
    Fly Away

I long to be the blue heron
        to stretch a drape of feathers
        across the orange window of sunrise

fall through drifts of wind
        perch in a weeping willow
        on a Wu Zhen canvas

rest against calligraphy poems
        on parchment scrolls with rolling hills
        native rivers and steepled mountains

make a home beside the Yellow Sea
        step through silent mists
        pour my plumed body

over scattered surf
        soundless as white foam pillows
        smoothing footprints in sand

        instead I am standing in a knob
        of tangled vines and stinging bees
        in a clattering city of rock salt
        the sky peppers with fumes
        humanity's tide crushes bone
        hollow as a bird's feather

Playing the Long Game
Inspired by W. S. Merwin's *Yesterday*

My friend says you were a good flight attendant
    I say yes   yes I was
she says all those miles you walked the people
you served that trash you picked up
    oh yes   I say
wasn't it difficult to be nice all the time
always smile
    I say yes   and smile
people can be cranky demanding
selfish drunk mean so talkative
    yes I say   I understand
she asks about retired life missing constant travel
what I did with my uniform
nowhere to go nothing to do how do I get along
    I glance at my watch
    hmm   I say
you must be bored and lonely she insists
watching TV all day
    I say nothing
    look out the screen door
    at a ruby-throated hummingbird

    canvas longs for impasto pigment
    the garden trellis for anxious sprays
        of rambling roses
    poetry deadlines clamor
    bubbly cobbler calls for blackberries
    valises await June's voyage to Venezuela
she says   we have so much time
let's go for coffee
    measuring the stress of her emptiness
    I say   yes
you're a good friend she says
    yes   yes

Smitten

> *Happiness sneaks in through a door you didn't*
> *know you left open.*
> —John Barrymore

The middle of this day, I find enjoyment
in a freshly-mopped cider-colored oak floor
and a cup of Earl Grey, tint of cream.

Evening finds me captivated with the McCalls—Mom,
Dad, and four little girls, Sophie just six months—
out for their after-dinner stroll, labs Polo and Tucker
bounding like out-of-control springs.

It's the best of delights—no covetous craving
or burning hunger, no possessiveness or suspicion.
These are instant attractions. Warmed by the jay
in his blue jacket, perched in the peach tree—
swept by beauty of a pink hydrangea blossom
big as my head—adoration of my gray tabby
who sleeps feet in the air and snores like a foghorn.

I figure I'm up to one hundred thousand moments
of pleasure. Not your passionate, moonstruck,
bend-me-backwards-and-ravish-me-ecstasy,
although there's been that, too.

These joys help knit me together, though I'm netted
with crazing, delicate as fine china or an old painting.
If a random arrow threatens to bury me,
I let the words catch the wind and burrow the air.

Tomorrow I will fall in love again as I meditate
to Mozart, feel compassion for the street musician
by the metro, and have gratitude for my roof
with its slate shingles. I could even forgive life's blows
as I barb the dirt and water forget-me-nots that will bloom,
affectionately, next spring.

Jesse

Golden Shovel* poem aprés W.S. Merwin's
Separation
Your absence has gone through me
Like thread through a needle.
Everything I do is stitched with its color.

Early spring no grass grows in your
mud-brown meadow. The absence
of life is dispiriting. A slow whinny has
whispered my name, wondered where I've gone.
Summoned from far-off places, I pass through
clouds until ground, solid underfoot, brings me
to the paddock. Our chestnut manes rise like
soft waves of heat. Haunches twitch as we thread
our way back to companionship through
breath, velvet muzzle to cheek, and a
pocketful of sugar cubes. The compass needle
of our bond points forward, everything
forgiven. Bareback, flying across pastures, I
nudge you to full gallop. We do
a slow dance at the tree line, continue until day is
short and skies are stitched
in patchwork pastels. Cantering home with
earthy musk perfuming air, its
scent enriches reunion. Evening changes color.

*The Golden Shovel form takes a line or lines
from another poem and uses each word in order
as the end word of each line in a new poem

Let's Seize the Day

Draped across my shoulder like a shawl,
you claim my pillow as your own.
Face nuzzles my neck, whiskers
scratch and flick along my ear. *Let's slouch*
I hear you say in a soft purr, *and disappear*
into the day. Let's lounge like lizards,
then chase butterflies. We'll collect
patches of sunshine that cross the Mojave,
sleep folded together, rising only
to drink and gorge. You go on,
presenting your plan in a fur-lined
jewel box.

I might be retired but still have work to do.
Rubbing the top of your head, I give it
a quick kiss. Morning reveille beckons
as my feet hit the floor. Charismatic, you leap
from bed, graceful as a dancer, and begin
to weave persuasive chatter with gentle
touch, charming as a magic spell.

I can't be a lazy sloth and stay home,
I laugh. You switch tactics, take on the alpha role.
Loudly but lovingly you demand breakfast,
lead me to the kitchen like I'm leashed.

Your maneuvers don't work, so you stand
directly in front of me with brazen assurance.
By accident I step on your tabby tail.
You screech like bad brakes on a car.

Still Life

I'm stopped at a red light when I see him,
downtown, late afternoon. He's sitting
on the steps of a building—a bank, I think.
Sun filtering through high-rises casts shadows
across his knees.

He leans against the hand rail, face in the sun,
just sitting, eyes open, staring. Not seeing,
just open and staring—an empty hourglass,
a human still life.

Green light, hazy through a tear, time to move on—
appointments to get oil changed, pick out wooden
shutters for windows, home to make Italian vegetable
soup. Better stop for fresh focaccia bread—number
six on this Tuesday's *To-Do* list.

Is the man homeless?
He seems to have vanished from the body.
Does he dream with his eyes wide open?
I have soup to warm me. Does he like soup?
I check my list again: call Lisa, wrap Jack's present,
sign up for spiritual retreat.

Tomorrow's list is twice as long.
What will the man do tomorrow?
Sit on another step
and stare, lost in a prison
of his own making?

I fill in lines on the page, horizontal bars.
This is my life, an activity prison.

Neighbors

The patriarch next door wields a Beretta—
he used to hit the bullseye
before Parkinson's disease hit him.

Mrs. Pierre's poodle
exercises eminent domain
in her Master's bedroom,
snoring allegretto.
Mr. Pierre, a tailspin
of resentment, sleeps in the guest room.

A gray-haired wife across the street
was punched by a stroke, paralyzed,
and moved into Assisted Living.
Her husband followed—
they assisted him with dying.

Gregory is a Times Square billboard,
model-handsome. His voice is a murmur
of the sea—his yard, loud as a pigsty.
With the attention span of a gnat,
he can't hold a job.

A set of twins are identical in looks only.
Three minutes older, Terry is the vena cava
of the pair, sucking air from her parents' dream.
Kerry is the aorta, bringing dawn to the sky.

Sam slithers to his sedan each morning
at 7:36, hissing at children walking to school,
coiling to strike if they step on his lawn.

A cadre of climbers rent the gray house
with black shutters. White winters
they camp in the fenced backyard,

rehearsing for Kilimanjaro.
They laugh off hypothermia.
But there is no refuge
from high-altitude cerebral edema,
malignant fate of fools.

Eddie follows in his brother's footsteps,
plunders the legs of insects and watches them
convulse. The brother is in prison for assault.
Their family Doberman is wild-eyed and vicious.

Passing the bathroom door, Judd's mom
is dry-mouthed as she glimpses her 16-year old
approaching manhood.

Riley is a bachelor. His wife discarded him like gum
under a seat. Now he lives inside his snow globe,
collecting dust like a knick-knack.

Valentina is a rhododendron, large and showy,
stabbing the air with her perfume. She blooms
in spring and tolerates her mate's shady habits.

The plastic surgeon is retired. He nurtures
pink rosebuds in the garden,
as soft as silicone C-cups.

Blackberries conquer the empty corner lot. Suzy,
born in the Year of the Tiger, feeds feral cats
that breed among the brambles.

Adelaide and Klaus met at Ellis Island. America's
crucible fused the teenagers together. Their marriage
is a thread of scarlet in a tapestry of immigrants.
Window box flowers growing from yesterday's storm.

Coffee Group

Bill moved to Colorado—we still talk about him,
even call on his birthday. Tree-trunk-shaped Scott
came and went quickly, a shaft of shadow.
We're down to four regulars after eighteen years,
vintage classics.

I'm the only cat at this dog party. No hugging,
just, *Hey, How ya doin',* and *See ya.*

John's thoughts curl inside himself
like a fiddlehead fern, then his eyebrows rise
in skeptical arches. Ideas intersect his mind
like the sun arcs across the sky. I hold
a lantern between panorama and close-up,
madness and possibility. David's face, flexible
as a melting Salvador Dali watch, stormy
as a bruised sunset, has a narrow green stare.
Twig-framed, angular Bob, a natural comedian
with jawbones sharp as trouser creases,
is the pescetarian among us.

No discussion's off limits: WikiLeaks, the price
of silver, spiritual Soul Travel, politics.
Coffee Group's heartbeat allows for opinions
with no one held hostage. The dogs don't growl,
the cat doesn't claw.

We nestle into the diner's womb
on the last Sunday of each month,
during the porcelain winter
and the yellow shell of summer. For hours,
laughter and swearing bleed into our table's
intimate air, like ink drops spread
into every angle and wrinkle of wet paper.

Coniferous Wisdom

Old-growth forests flourish in a narrow
coastal zone. I've come to rest in the stillness
of nature, to learn among the toadstools
and branches twisted in supplication.
Towering ancients whisper through pine needles,
quiet as youth caught sharing secrets in class.
Moist moss covers bedrock bones, rooftops
of fairy abodes. I sense a small darkness
begin to loosen in the wild, wet shade.

Woodland sprites speak of ground soggy
as a sponge from ten feet of rain each year.
They tell me of blending beauty
and a rutted-bark money tree that drops
membranous gold in fall, raining coins
upon prick-eared red foxes painted in silhouette,
scurrying among scaly hemlocks.

Edible calendula and pansies with bewitching
hues of orange and violet dress, sprout
in sun and shower-drenched pockets
amid the imposing giants. Pitch and lacy patterns
are Victoria Secret's organic covers.

With silvery sharpness in the air, vines share tales
of moon and water. When the deluge comes,
I want to capture the sky's cleansing flood
in metal-banded oak barrels to rinse my hair.

I sleep with tent flap open to breathe
the sweet scent of fallen leaves. Tomorrow
may uncover more mysteries of the spruce
and fir. Old-growth forests are timberlands
of hoary wisdom.

Tell Me About the Ocean, She Asks

How can I describe the sea
to one who has never seen it?

Shades and smells, textures and tastes.
The way saltwater stings eyes,
dries crusty on skin,
how I can never get all the sand
out of my towel or shoes.
How the sound of waves
soothes crying babies
and anguished souls.

Where to start detailing colors
of water? Some days Roman-bath green,
cobalt or vivid aquamarine, emerald tinges.
Overcast days, translucent gray,
speckled and foamed.

The way gulls circle and dip,
then resettle on the beach,
all facing the same direction
like an audience at a play.
Sandpipers' forked feet
flit the waterline.

A girl's hair whips about her face,
a scarf ribbons behind her
as her smile chronicles the afternoon.
Sand castles appear and disappear,
sculpted by children inside fantasy worlds,
where impossibility can't exist.
Nearby, mothers live
in paperbacks,
reality as hazy
as their day at the beach.

Surf daubs the grainy shore
with bubbles. Prismatic tide pools
expose mussels, starfish, anemone.
Lichens spread spindly twig arms
across barnacles. Thick smells of fish,
taste of salt on lips.
Seaweed's kelp fingers
tangle among shore rocks
the way our lives intertwine.

How can I explain the way
the sun here is different
from inland sun,
turns skin rosy or golden,
reflects off breakers
that scatter into liquid diamonds?
The way the sea
wears calm or angry faces,
and is pulled by tides,
the way emotions
rise and fall,
ebb and flow,

and how it never stops moving
or changing—
primordial, ancient—
like time, like us.

My Promiscuous Muse

You sat with a silent stare last night,
begging recognition. I ignored you,
so you slipped away,
went to visit *Billy* back east.
He doesn't need you,
he's already been Poet Laureate.
But, being polite, he gives you attention,
dotes on your every word

while at home I storm and strut,
annoyed with your incessant
Billy this, Billy that.
I mourn our wasted hours,
our tempest-days.

If only you had gone to see
one of your sisters, to play
music with Euterpe, laugh with Thalia.
But no, you, Erato, wander, unfaithful.

What must I do to woo you back?
Slide down a rainbow?
Run down the north wind?
An elegant new journal waits, quill pen
slipped between unmarked pages,
fresh flowers in the celadon vase,
vanilla-scented taper in the candlestick.
All for you, Muse of lyric poetry.

Come home, tender beauty.
I pledge my heart, renew my vow,
shower you with chocolate
while we dance through the night.
Surely *Billy* would be too tired to tango.

Burden of Youth

I speak the truth, not so much as I would,
but as much as I dare, and I dare a little
more as I grow older.
—Montaigne

We start with breathing.
Apparently I've done it wrong
for sixty-four years.

Yoga instructors,
slight as a calligraphy stroke,
move through postures.
Asanas, they call them: Sun Salutations,
Cobra, Tree Pose, Down Dog. At twenty-one,
I too was a graceful, lithesome,
gazelle-like creature. Concave stomach,
twiggy thighs, no breasts.

I retain the grace, but now have crescent hips
and new-moon curves where there used to be abs.
Life experience and wisdom reveal
a well-rounded Soul.

My knees are too tender for Lotus,
but I can still twist from the waist
and bend like a triangle,
hands flat on the floor.

Warrior Two, with a lunge
and outstretched arms, is my favorite pose.
With flexibility of the young and strength
of the seasoned soldier,
I would not trade places
with one who has no lines on the face.

New Bearings

Let this be the last one—
the last poem I write about my sister,
the *psycho bulldog,* as I label her.
I need themes that don't have
shards of glass embedded in lines—
new verses about moonlight, music,
meadowlarks and tigers, even
French-press coffee.

Emotions clog my pen at midnight,
eject like ink from cuttlefish.
Blots appear in black hissing notes
like Medusa and her sisters, snakes for hair.
A glance can turn me to stone. My words,
rocks pelting a page, try to smash
the Pandora box of her heart—

         but I'm tired. Tired of revisiting
childhood cruelty, that old plough horse
with a heavy harness. Tired of plodding
the wedged and graveled path of wrongs.

By dawn, the angry sea has drained dry,
replaced by a bit of sadness
that she will no longer be a muse.

         I bury her. My compass
spins free, begins to navigate
a canopy of stars.

Yard Sale

The garage is full of stories, spicy condiments,
savory memories: Peruvian carved gourds,
copper pots from Mexico, Turkish kilim rugs.
At the bazaar, the shopkeeper's lower lip smirked
when my friend threw herself on a stack of carpets
to feel texture. It wasn't a possible sale
I saw in his smile.

Next to dad's stationary bike sit paintings
of the Eiffel Tower, the Sydney Opera House.
Machu Picchu—another home had cathedral ceilings
with museum-sized wall space. An embroidered cushion
depicting four-masted windjammer *Fantome*—
lost at sea the year after my cruise—
sits beside mom's turkey roaster.

A tail broken off a wooden horse
bought in Thailand—never glued back on.
One of those pincushions from Korea
with figures of Asian women,
arms stretched over the red hump where pins go.

A cardboard box with ponchos, saris, and kimonos
pitches over when I pile it on the side to sell.
His letters from Saigon scatter,
along with forty-five years of loss.
A blue bag opens—the ring dangles
from a tarnished silver chain,
a circle of backwater. One diamond is missing
from a bent bezel, the engraving still visible,

~ *Forever* ~

He never came home from Vietnam.
I've never forgotten those dark eyes, never
stopped wondering what could have been.

Mass for the Reverent Corpus

Selah!

My body is a cathedral. Worship here.
I am your blessing, your ablution, your hymn,
the bread and the wine. Gathering winds blow you
like a tempest to this house of god. Find sanctuary
and faith to fill your firmament. Prostrate yourself
with passion before my altar. Choir voices rise
as you cover me with a velvet vestment of skin.

Light a candle, pray for showers of forgiveness.
Your body, a seraph, flies to me. Our hosannas
greet frescoed saints. Alleluias and amazing grace
are the light in stained glass windows.
We stoke the fire of sensuous communion
ordained by holy order. My hunger
knows your taste. I smolder,
then burn with intoxicating incense.

Glowing chandeliers outline your head
like a halo. Arms, protective as angels' wings,
offer a mantilla of caresses. Anointed lips drink
from the chalice of desire. Be my devotion
and my shepherd. Comfort me.

Extol the body, entwined and spread
as on a cross, consecrated as any cathedral.

Rapture resounds while the celebrant intones
sanctus et benedictus. Shed your garments.

Come,
worship here.

The Night I Die

I think my last day comes in early October.
Muted morning gives way to faint light
that blanches windows. Clouds of rippled silk
striate the sky.

Air tastes cold and draws me like an ancient ache.
Remaining aspen leaves fall, dapple grass.
Children in the park bend like saplings. I pedal home,
prop my bike against the side of the garage,
catch scents of cinnamon and wild honey.

A puppet pulled by strings, I walk the hall,
glance at a world map dense with pins
for places I've visited. Things I hunger for are gone.
I am the wing of a white bird.

Weight of the past disappears quick as a minnow
in a creek. I nap curled on my left side, wrist angled
under my chin, dreaming of feathers. Afternoon rain
puddles ground, washes the wind.

From the back porch, a paper lantern sun sinks.
Iris-blue tops a kaleidoscope alive with layers
of burnt orange and saffron. Crimson reflects
on the bay window like a soft scarf.

Rings catch pink rays, carry memories
thick with love. He was the color of wood smoke
after sickness leached warmth from his skin.

Silence spins out as street lamps glow.
Sunset's purple robes cloak the sky,
comforting as velvet. Violet streaks
stair step to heaven and stars
sprinkle pinpoints of light.
I hear him call my name.

Crosswinds

Thirty-five years, no, closer to forty,
the world is mine—business in Barcelona,
trekking in Katmandu, dining in Dubai.
Sundays in Seoul, Fridays in Frankfurt,
Tuesdays in Thailand. Wednesdays,
who knows where? In perpetual motion,
I come and go like the tide.

Now, the scent of coconut curry with cardamom
and coriander wafts from my own kitchen
instead of a New Delhi diner.

Flower beds with daisies and dahlias
rival gardens at Buckingham Palace—
okay, not exactly, but frenzied freesias
spill over the walk leading to my front door.

Time flows like a slow, silent river. The cats
never answer the doorbell, too lazy to open
an eye. Sometimes, breakfast is past noon.

I'm as intoxicated with my bungalow
as a honeybee in a field of bluebells—
besotted with the chintz sofa, smitten with sleep
on the king-size four poster, possessed by pleasure
swinging in the sisal hammock.

No more red-eyes to Rome, headwinds
in Havana, tailwinds in Trinidad. No pressure.
No crosswinds. Just a place to lounge
on a covered porch—a cotton candy place
to snap a wishbone, put landing gear down,
and taxi home.

Judge Comments:

"The whole work is a gift. Experiences in the wider world have been internalized by the poet, and inasmuch as they have been shared through the poems, we, too, have made them our own, part of us. We end the book, home from a similar journey lived vicariously through the writing. The poet takes us with her. The humble beginning mentioned in the first poem, and the precious simplicity of the life described in the last poem, which still feels very personal, saves the book from the risk of being pretentious, prevents the poems from coming across as a boastful display of exotic locales and esoteric experiences. No matter who we are, we can relate. The release from the hustle and bustle of the jet set life, the release from the business of the poems and their adventures, perhaps in a way, gratitude for all the fully lived years—even challenges celebrated as part of the wonder of life—and a peaceful acceptance at the end of life itself, all seem captured in the culminating image of ceasing crosswinds. We end as satisfied, perhaps, as the poet herself.

"The work seems 'finished'. The title grabs attention, and the book has good cohesion around that title (without all being about exactly the same thing). Everything fits, the title, the opening quote, the very creative section titles (love them), and closing with the title poem. There's an additional sense and sensation you get when reading the whole work through, not just the odd poem within. Kudos on that. The book does what a good individual poem does, it covers a lot of ground in relatively few words. We know where the author came from, where she went, and where she ended up. I love the title poem and what it has to say, and the whole book testifies of its message. The writer's life has come full circle, and so has the collection. (P.S. I cried twice reading your touching poems. Well done!)

"I said I think that everyone can relate to your poems. But then again, I'm also a world traveler / world citizen from humble beginnings. The whole book functions like the pieces of an extended metaphor. We finally see at the end what the poet has teased us with from the very front cover and throughout. I like how an end to the crosswinds of life is also an end to *Crosswinds* the book."

About the Judge:

Beverly Monestier (Nikolaus) is published and awarded in both poetry and prose, and is the author of two books of poetry, *Modern Ruins,* published with support from the Ministry of Education and Culture in the Republic of Cyprus, and *What the House Is Made Of,* the 2009 Edwin Eakin Book Award Winner. She's taught writing, poetry performance, and creativity. Beverly is currently working on publications related to her professional endeavors in the field of human development, especially work with people in crisis, who've been traumatized, and those with a family member (past or present) suffering from a porn/sexual addiction, a true epidemic today, even among our youth. "It is incredibly fulfilling at this stage in my life to be called to use my writing talents for such an important cause."

About the Poet

Anita Krotz was born in La Jolla, California and raised in Pasadena, California where she attended Pasadena City College, started a photography business, won awards for her work, and had a photograph published on the cover of a Pan American World Airways travel magazine. Her sophomore year was spent at San Diego State College. Anita has a Bachelor's degree in Political Science from the University of California, Los Angeles.

Prior to her life profession, she had many enjoyable jobs: playground coach for elementary school students; legal secretary for an attorney in Beverly Hills; Hogle Zoo docent. Anita had a rewarding career as an International Flight Attendant for thirty-five years, starting with Western Airlines in 1974 and retiring from Delta Airlines after the merger of the two companies. She is a gourmet cook and between flight assignments worked part-time as a prep chef.

She has lived in Los Angeles, San Diego, and Lake Tahoe, California; Seattle, Washington; Portland, Oregon; New York City; and Park City, Utah where she enjoyed riding her quarter horse, Jesse, over the Wasatch Range. Time was spent living in Antigua, Guatemala where she studied Spanish and became a language-speaker for Western, flying to various cities in Mexico. Salt Lake City, Utah is her current home.

While flying for a major airline and traveling the world, she acquired a private pilot's license. After retirement from her full-time occupation as a Delta crew member, she worked part-time as a bartender at an airline premium flyer lounge.

Anita is passionate about the study of spirit through Eckankar, the Path of Spiritual Freedom. She has a story published in one of their books and volunteered services as CFO for the local chapter.

Writing helps to work through life's ever changing identities. Poetry has become an even stronger way to express the complexity of human experience. The Utah State Poetry Society is a supportive organization that has enhanced her study of this rewarding process. She has won more than 135 awards in state and national contests, was the Editor for the Utah State Poetry Society's 2013 edition of *Panorama*, as well as a judge for the Redrock Writers' Seminar contest published in *Chaparral Poetry Forum, 2016*. She was a proofreader for a spiritually-themed book by author M. Harrington. Poems have been generated by her younger years, growing up, career, retirement, and the broad world around her.

She is certified as a Master Gardener growing vegetables, fruit, herbs, and flowers. She was taught to sew by her grandmother. This was a valuable skill while making several hundred quilts for a local children's hospital.

Current activities include volunteer work as an usher for a local playhouse, making hand-built clay dishes, and fine art painting. Anita is a gallery-level artist with an art gallery showing in April, 2017.

Anita still travels widely, both flying and cruising, and often visits family in California. During the writing of this volume of poetry she lived with two cherished cats, Zeke and Zena. They both passed on after nearly 20 years of life together. She loved them dearly and misses them very much.

Previous Utah State Poetry Society Poets of the Year

**Deceased

1965 ** Vesta P. Crawford, *Short Grass Woman*
1966 ** Lael W. Hill, *A Legacy of Years*
1967 ** Berta H. Christensen, *Walk the Proud Morning*
1968 ** Betty W. Madsen, *The Amaranth*
1969 ** J. A. Christensen, *The Deep Song*
1970 ** Max Golightly, *A Morning of Taurus*
1971 ** Alice Morrey Bailey, *Eden from an Apple Seed*
1972 ** Maxine R. Jennings, *A Lamp to Shine*
1973   Geraldine R. Pratt, *Bell on the Wind*
1974 ** LeRoy Burke Meagher, *Beyond This Hour*
1975 ** Helen Mar Cook, *Shape of Flight*
1976 ** Caroline Eyring Miner, *Lasso the Sunrise*
1977   Clarence P. Socwell, *Intrinsic Tapestries*
1978 ** Pearle M. Olsen, *Frame the Laced Moments*
1979   Randall L. Hall, *Mosaic*
1980 ** LaVerde Morgan Clayson, *Furrows of Renewal*
1981   Frank M. Decaria, *Songs Within the Sounds*
1982 ** LaVon B. Carroll, *The Shrouded Carousel*
1983 ** Bonnie Howe Behunin, *Wake the Unicorn*
1984   Joyce Ellen Davis, *In Willy's House*
1985 ** Patricia S. Grimm, *Timepiece*
1986   Dorothy Logan, *Child in a Sculptured Bowl*
1987   Kathryn Clement, *Riddlestone*
1988 ** Sherwin W. Howard, *Sometime Voices*
1989 ** Maryan Paxton, *Downwind Toward Night*
1990   Elaine Christensen, *At the Edges*
1991   Robert Joseph Frederickson, *Being Here*
1992   Brad Roghaar, *Unraveling the Knot*
1993   Margaret Pettis, *Chokecherry Rain*

1994   Muriel Heal Bywater, *Stretching Toward Wild Swans*
1995 ** Elaine L. Ipson, *Where Ghosts Are Garrisoned*
1996   Nancy Hanks Baird, *The Shell in Silk*
1997   Marilyn Darley Williams, *The Red Rooster Cafe*
1998   Mikal Lofgren, *Trudi Smiles Back*
1999   Marilyn Bushman-Carlton, *Cheat Grass*
2000   Kolette Montague, *Easing Into Light*
2001   Rita Bowles, *God in Assorted Boxes*
2002 ** Evelyn Hughes, *Furnace of Affliction*
2003   Judy Johns, *If I Could Speak in Silk*
2004   Maurine Haltiner, *A Season and a Time*
2005   T. Kevin Clark, *Song of an Oquirrh Son*
2006   Sue Ranglack, *Shouting from the Book of Orange*
2007   N. Colwell Snell, *Hand Me My Shadow*
2008 ** Helen Keith Beaman, *Edges Disappear*
2009   Gail G. Schimmelpfennig, *The Frozen Kingdom*
2010   Rosalyn Whitaker Ostler, *Walking the Earth Barefoot*
2011   Lee C. Snell, *Night Wind Home*
2012   Dawnell H. Griffin, *On Judgment Day*
2013   Jon Sebba, *Yossi, Yasser, & Other Soldiers*
2014   Joyce Webb Kohler, *like water, like bread*
2015   Candy Lish Fowler, *On a Road that Knows Me*
2016   Duane T. Rygh, *My Bright Red Scream*

About the UTSPS Book Award

In 1965, Nicholas Morgan and Paul Pehrson established a revolving fund to publish a book by the person whom the Utah State Poetry Society, following a statewide contest, designated Utah Poet of the Year. As costs increased, the Society, assisted by the Utah Arts Council, supplemented the fund. In 1985, Pearle M. Olsen, the 1978 recipient, donated a large sum to assist the project. Subsequently, Mrs. Olsen's children, John K.M. Olsen, Billye O. Jenkins, and Carlyle O. Morris, made further contributions to ensure continuation of the project.

In 2011, substantial donations to the Poetry Society from the Johnson Family, the Hanks Family, and other friends allowed this well-loved project to continue. The name was changed to the Utah State Poetry Society Book Publication Award to reflect this new sponsorship.

Anita M. Krotz's book, *Crosswinds,* is the fifty-third volume in this valuable series.

Awards and Publication

Pg. 14: *Two Hundred Billion Stars Away* won First HM, UTSPS 2014 and Fifth HM, NFSPS 2017

Pg. 15: *Rainy Day Memory* won Third Place, UTSPS 2006; Published Panorama 2006

Pg. 16: *Horse of the Muses* won Second Place, UTSPS 2010; Published Panorama 2013

Pg. 17: *Fifth Grade* won Second HM, NFSPS 2016

Pg. 18: *In the End It Is More Mysterious Than Life Itself* won First Place, NFSPS 2012; Published Encore 2012

Pg. 19: *Set Free* won Third Place, UTSPS 2016

Pg. 22: *Aftershocks* won First Place, UTSPS 2016

Pg. 23: (A version of) *Unfaithful Moon* won First Place, UTSPS 2015

Pg. 24: *About-Face* won Second Place, NFSPS 2015 and prior to publication won Second Place, UTSPS 2016; Published Encore 2015

Pg. 25: *Last Rites* won Third Place, UTSPS 2011

Pg. 26: *Flaming Candles* won First Place, UTSPS 2013

Pg. 32: *Career at 35,000 Feet* won Second HM, UTSPS 2016

Pg. 34: *Parselmouth* won Second Place, UTSPS 2017

Pg. 35: (A version of) *Ritual* won Third Place, UTSPS 2014

Pg. 37: *It's All for the Birds* won Second Place, UTSPS 2017

Pg. 38: *October Cups a Sparkler in My Hands* won Third Place, NFSPS 2017; Published Encore 2017

Pg. 39: *Alaska Is a Grizzly* is a version of *Disappearing Wilderness* which won Third Place, IFSPS 2008 and was published in Panorama, 2009

Pg. 41: *Alps of Adversity* won First Place, NFSPS 2010; Published Encore 2010; Published Panorama 2011

Pg. 42: *Yellow* won Second HM, UTSPS 2015 and Second HM, NFSPS 2016

Pg. 43: *Call of the Celts* won Seventh HM, NFSPS 2016

Pg. 44: *Rising Sun* won Second Place, UTSPS 2014 and Second Place, NFSPS 2016; Published Encore 2016

Pg. 45: *Ten Cents a Bloom* won Third HM, UTSPS 2014

Pg. 46: (A version of) *Le Mont-Saint-Michel* won First HM, UTSPS 2011; Version in book won First Place, UTSPS 2014 and First Place, NFSPS 2014; Published Encore 2014

Pg. 47: *Wake of the Wind* won Second Place, UTSPS 2016 and Seventh HM, NFSPS 2016

Pg. 48: (A version of) *The Letter* won Third Place, NFSPS 2007; Published Encore 2007; Published Panorama 2008

Pg. 51: *Love Bears Me Home* won Special Recognition, UTSPS 2013

Pg. 53: *Fly Away Fly Away* won Second Place, UTSPS 2014

Pg. 54: *Playing the Long Game* won Second Place NFSPS 2017; Published Encore 2017

Pg. 55: *Smitten*, under the title *Falling In Love* won First Place, UTSPS 2013

Pg. 56: *Jesse* won Third HM, UTSPS 2017

Pg. 58: (A version of) *Still Life* won First Place, UTSPS 2006 under the title *Human Still Life*; Published Panorama 2006

Pg. 59: *Neighbors* won Third Place, UTSPS 2013 under the title *Neighborhood Oddities*

Pg. 62: (A version of) *Coniferous Wisdom* won First Place, IFSPS 2008; Published Panorama 2010

Pg. 63: *Tell Me About the Ocean, She Asks* won Third Place, NFSPS 2010; Published Encore 2010

Pg. 65: *My Promiscuous Muse* won Third Place, UTSPS 2010

Pg. 66: (A version of) *Burden of Youth* won Third Place, UTSPS 2010; Published Panorama 2010

Pg. 67: *New Bearings* won First Place, UTSPS 2014, and Fourth HM, NFSPS 2014, and First Place, NFSPS 2015; Published Encore 2015

Pg. 68: *Yard Sale* won Second HM, UTSPS 2014

Pg. 69: *Mass for the Reverent Corpus* won Third HM, UTSPS 2011 and Third Place, NFSPS 2015; Published Encore 2015

Pg. 70: *The Night I Die* won Second Place, UTSPS 2014

Pg. 71: The poem, *Crosswinds*, under the original title of *No More Red-Eyes*, won Special Recognition, UTSPS 2013; Second HM, UTSPS 2014; and Special Recognition, UTSPS 2015

Prior to winning First Place in 2017, the manuscript *Crosswinds*, under the original title of *No More Red-Eyes,* won Third Place, UTSPS Manuscript Contest, 2013, Judge: Rob Carney; Third Honorable Mention, UTSPS Manuscript Contest, 2014, Judge: Susan Elizabeth Howe; Third Place, UTSPS Manuscript Contest, 2015, Judge: January Gill O'Neil; and Second Place, UTSPS Manuscript Contest, 2016, Judge: Jeremy M. Downes.